Presents

Kerry Burton-Galley
is a writer, artist, and animal rights activist.
She lives with her husband, Nigel,
and their Thai rescue dog,
nestled between the Moors and the Dales.

What the Sky Would Tell You

Sky Facts for Kind and Curious Little Minds

Copyright © 2025 Kerry Burton-Galley
Copyright © 3 Gargoyles Publishing
Cover image and illustrations
Copyright © Kerry Burton-Galley

The right of Kerry Burton-Galley to be identified as the author
of this work has been asserted by her in accordance
with section 77 and 78 of the Copyright,
Designs and Patents Act, 1988.
All rights reserved.

No part of this publication may be reproduced or transmitted
or utilized in any form or by any means
(electronic, mechanical, photocopying or otherwise)
without permission in writing from the publisher.

ISBN: 978-1-0684629-5-5

This is a work of creative non-fiction.
The events portrayed are to the best of the author's memory.
However, names, places and other details have either been
altered or omitted entirely in order to protect the privacy
of the people involved.

FACT
Some Birds Can Fly Above the Clouds!

Some birds are amazing high-flyers. Eagles, albatrosses — and especially bar-headed geese — can soar so high they glide above stormy skies and even over the tallest mountains in the world!

FACT
Many Stars Are Suns!

Lots of stars you see in the night sky are actually distant suns — some much bigger or smaller than ours, shining from far, far away.

FACT
The Sky Helps Create the Seasons!

The Earth is a little tilted as it spins around the sun. Because of that, different places get different amounts of sunlight during the year — and that's what makes the seasons change!

FACT
Lightning is Hotter Than the Sun!

A single bolt of lightning is much hotter than than the surface of the sun. It heats the air around it super fast — so fast that it makes a big boom called thunder!

FACT

The Sky Tells Baby Birds When to Hatch!

Sunlight shining through the eggshell helps baby birds know when it's time to hatch. The sky's light acts like a gentle signal — letting them know the world is ready to meet them.

FACT
The Sky is a Map for Migrating Birds!

Many birds travel thousands of miles each year along invisible sky-paths called flyways. They use the sun, stars, and wind to guide them — like a built-in compass passed down from bird to bird, generation after generation. The sky shows them the way home.

PROBLEM
The Sky is Getting Hot and Wild!

When people burn things like petrol and gas — or raise lots of animals on farms — it makes the Earth, and the skies above it, warmer than they should be. As the planet heats up, we're seeing stronger storms, more wildfires, and strange weather that's harder to predict.

WHAT CAN WE DO TO HELP?
Help the Sky Stay Cool!

We can help by using less energy, planting trees, and choosing kinder foods — like yummy plant-based meals instead of meat, dairy and egg ones. These small changes help clean the air, cool the sky, and protect animals, people, and our planet.

PROBLEM
The Night Sky is Disappearing!

In many places, bright city lights shine all night long — so brightly that stars can't be seen anymore. This is called light pollution, and it confuses birds, bats, bugs, and many more that rely on the stars and moon to find their way.

HOW CAN WE HELP?
Let the Stars Shine Again!

We can help by turning off lights we don't need at night and avoid using any lights outside our homes. If we keep the sky darker, more animals can find their way — and we get to see the stars sparkle again!

PROBLEM
The Sky's Protective Blanket is Wearing Thin!

High above the clouds is a special part of the sky called the ozone layer. It acts like a blanket, protecting the Earth from the sun's strongest rays. But certain gases — from sprays and pollution — have damaged it in places, making it thin.

WHAT CAN WE DO TO HELP?
Protect the Sky's Blanket!

We can help the ozone layer by choosing natural, planet-friendly sprays and cleaners, and by using less energy. Many of the worst gases have already been banned — but we can still do our part to keep the sky safe, strong, and protective for everyone!

FACT
Butterflies Sense the Sky with Their Antennae!
Butterflies don't just use their eyes — they have special sensors in their antennae to help track the sun and keep their direction when flying.

FACT
Trees Talk Through the Air!
When a tree is hurt or attacked by insects, it can release tiny chemicals into the air. Nearby trees "smell" the warning and get ready to protect themselves — it's like trees sending messages on the wind!

FACT
The Sun Powers the Planet!
The sun gives energy to plants, warms the land, air, and sea, and even helps create wind and rain. Without the sun, there would be no weather and no food — it's our planet's greatest power source!

FACT
The Wind Helps New Things to Grow!
Some seeds, like dandelions and spinning sycamore seeds, are shaped perfectly to catch the wind. Air currents lift them up and carry them far away, helping new plants grow in new places — like tiny travellers on sky journeys!

FACT
Elephants Use the Sky to Find Water!
Elephants lift their trunks high into the air to sniff the sky. They can smell rain from over 100 miles away — and often walk for days to find it.

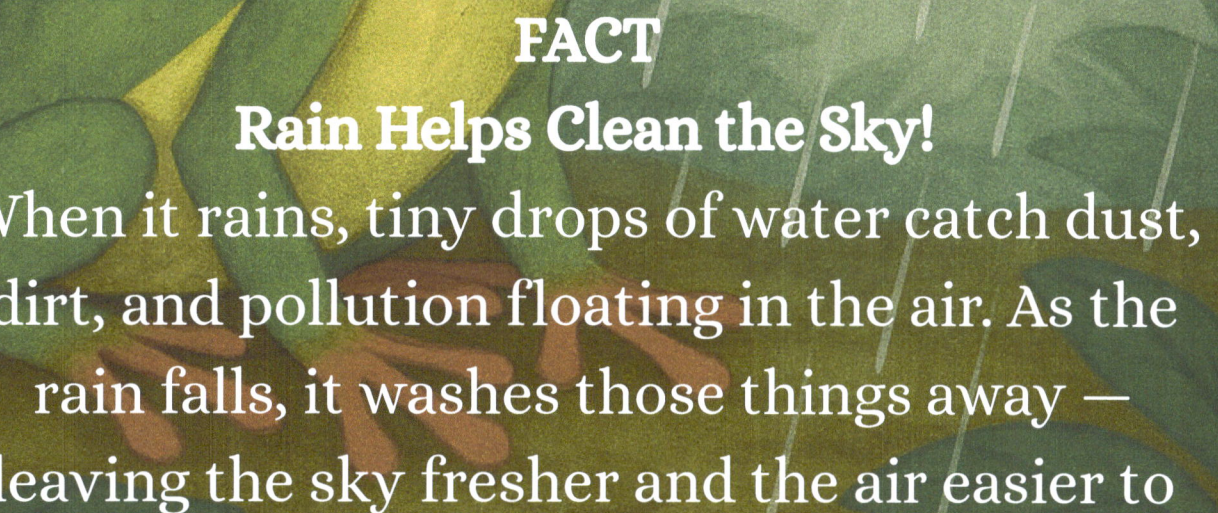

FACT
Rain Helps Clean the Sky!
When it rains, tiny drops of water catch dust, dirt, and pollution floating in the air. As the rain falls, it washes those things away — leaving the sky fresher and the air easier to breathe.

Thank You for Helping the Sky!

50p from every book you buy will go to real-life sky protectors —

the **International Dark-Sky Association!**

They work to protect the night sky and stop it from being taken over by bright lights.

By keeping things dark, they help bats, birds, bugs, and other animals that need moonlight and stars to find their way.

By choosing this book, you've already made a difference — thank you for being a sky hero!

ACKNOWLEDGEMENTS

Nigel, you are the calm in every storm. You never stopped believing — in these books, or in me. Thank you for your childlike enthusiasm and your grounding love that holds me steady.
You gave this book its wings.

www.ingramcontent.com/pod-product-compliance
Lightning Source LLC
Chambersburg PA
CBHW042053030526
44119CB00062B/496